CLASSIFIED

Civil War

SPIES

BY CRAIG SODARO

Consultant:
Jan Goldman, EdD
Founding Board Member
International Intelligence Ethics Association
Washington, D.C.

Velocity Books are published by Capstone Press,
1710 Roe Crest Drive, North Mankato, Minnesota 56003
www.capstonepub.com

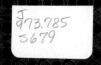

Library of Congress Cataloging-in-Publication Data
Sodaro, Craig.
Civil War spies / by Craig Sodaro.
pages cm. — (Velocity. Classified)
Includes bibliographical references and index.
ISBN 978-1-4296-9976-1 (library binding)
ISBN 978-1-4765-3584-5 (ebook PDF)
1. United States—History—Civil War, 1861-1865—Secret service—Juvenile literature. 2. United States—History—Civil War, 1861-1865—Underground movements—Juvenile literature. 3. Spies—United States—History—19th century. 4. Spies—Confederate States of America—History. I. Title.
E608.S685 2014
973.7'85—dc23

2013009488

Editorial Credits
Mandy Robbins, editor; Veronica Scott, designer; Jennifer Walker, production specialist

Photo Credits
Alamy: North Wind Picture Archives, 4-5, 32; Corbis, 21 (top); Courtesy of the Navy Art Collection, Washington, D.C., 24-25; CriaImages.com: Jay Robert Nash Collection, 36; Historical Photograph Collection/lh110, Digital Library and Archives, University Libraries, Virginia Tech, 13; Kansas State Historical Society, 23; Library of Congress: Brady-Handy Collection, 7, 39, 44 (left), Civil War Collection, 9, 19, 33, 44 (right), Morgan Collection of Civil War drawings, 40-41; National Archives and Records Administration, 26-27, 44-45; Newscom: akg-images, 34-35, C.D. Fredricks Picture History, 15, E. and H.T. Anthony Picture History, 30, Mathew Brady Picture History, 17; Shutterstock: 4736202690, 22, Jeff Kinsey, 43, Katherine Campbell, 31, Neveshkin Nikolay, 5 (inset), rick seeney, cover, Sandra Matic, 42-43, Stephanie Frey, 42; Wikimedia, 10, 18, 21 (bottom), 28, 29

Artistic Effects
Shutterstock

Printed in the United States of America in North Mankato, Minnesota.
032013   007223CGF13

TABLE OF CONTENTS

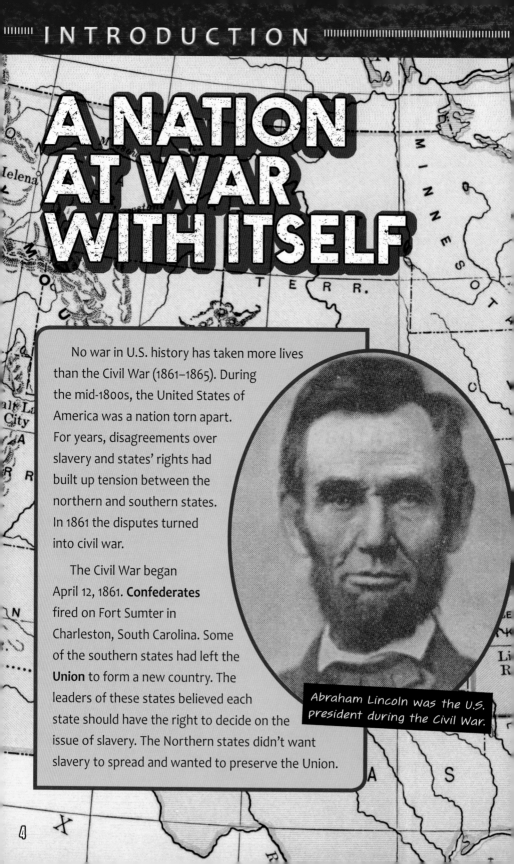

A NATION AT WAR WITH ITSELF

No war in U.S. history has taken more lives than the Civil War (1861–1865). During the mid-1800s, the United States of America was a nation torn apart. For years, disagreements over slavery and states' rights had built up tension between the northern and southern states. In 1861 the disputes turned into civil war.

The Civil War began April 12, 1861. **Confederates** fired on Fort Sumter in Charleston, South Carolina. Some of the southern states had left the **Union** to form a new country. The leaders of these states believed each state should have the right to decide on the issue of slavery. The Northern states didn't want slavery to spread and wanted to preserve the Union.

Abraham Lincoln was the U.S. president during the Civil War.

SPYING IN THE CIVIL WAR

When the war began, the U.S. government had no official organizations for spying. The Central Intelligence Agency (CIA) and Federal Bureau of Investigation (FBI) did not exist. The North and South had to find ways to sneak messages to and from their armies. One spy hid messages in her hair. Others wrote messages in code. Many spies used acting talents to create characters. One pretended to be a crazy old lady wandering the streets of the Confederate capital, Richmond, Virginia.

How did spies get their information? They eavesdropped on conversations. Some spies were friends with powerful officials. These officials didn't realize their "friends" were sending information to the other side. Newspapers printed stories about upcoming troop movements. These papers were **smuggled** across enemy lines so commanders would know what the other side was doing. More than anything, Civil War spies were resourceful. By thinking quickly on their feet, they were able to influence the events of the war.

Confederate—a person who supported the cause of the Confederate States of America
Union—the United States of America; also the Northern states that fought against the Southern states in the Civil War
smuggle—to bring something or someone into or out of a country illegally

SPY RING LEADER

On a hot July afternoon in 1861, Betty Duvall passed a Union roadblock into Virginia. There the teenager changed into riding clothes and borrowed a horse. She rode on to a small Confederate **post**. She approached the tent of the commanding officer and told him she had a message for General G. T. Beauregard.

Betty pulled out a small silk purse that had been hidden inside her hair. In the purse was a coded message. When decoded it read, "McDowell has certainly been ordered to advance on the sixteenth. R.O.G."

The message warned the Confederates that the Union army would attack soon. Knowing this, the Southerners were prepared. They defeated the Union troops at the Battle of Bull Run, the first major battle of the Civil War.

"R.O.G" stood for Rose O'Neal Greenhow. Mrs. Greenhow lived in Washington, D.C., which was held by the Union. She was wealthy and knew many Union leaders. Rose had agreed to help Lieutenant Colonel Thomas Jordan set up a Confederate **spy ring** in the Union's capital. Jordan taught Rose a 26-symbol **cipher** to send messages. She passed along information during the early years of the war. Brave messengers such as Betty Duvall carried Rose's messages to Confederate leaders.

Rose Greenhow and her daughter embrace outside Old Capitol Prison, where Rose was held in 1862.

post—a military base where soldiers are stationed or trained
spy ring—a group of spies working together for a common goal
cipher—a code that uses letters or symbols to represent letters of the alphabet

SCHOOL PRINCIPAL SPY

Thomas Conrad was the school principal of Georgetown Institute, a school for boys in Washington, D.C. Many times throughout 1861, he stood at his office window that looked down at the Potomac River. The river separated Washington, D.C., from the Confederate state of Virginia. By raising and lowering his window shades, Conrad would send messages to Confederate soldiers on the other side of the river.

Thomas Conrad was not just a headmaster. He was a spy. Thomas had been born 24 years earlier in Virginia. He firmly believed the Southern states had the right to form a new country.

Since he lived in the North, Thomas learned where the Union camps were located. He heard talk about when and where soldiers would move. Being a Southern supporter, he passed this information to the Confederate soldiers on the other side of the river.

At graduation ceremonies in 1861, Thomas and many of his students did not hide their Southern sympathies. Students gave speeches supporting the Confederacy. The band played "Dixie," the Confederate anthem.

Union soldiers guard the Potomac River across from Washington, D.C.

Old Capitol Prison, 1800s

FACT:

Old Capitol Prison was once a fashionable boarding house just east of the Capitol building. By 1861 it was used as a prison for spies and captured soldiers.

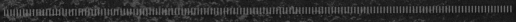

Later in the summer of 1861, Thomas was arrested for working for the Confederates. He was sent to the Old Capitol Prison in Washington, D.C., but was released in a prisoner exchange. Thomas immediately headed to Richmond, Virginia, the Confederate capital.

Thomas enlisted in the 3rd Virginia **Cavalry** as a **chaplain** and also served as a spy in Washington, D.C. Union soldiers wouldn't suspect a chaplain of being a spy. Thomas could pass through enemy lines more easily than a regular soldier or **civilian**. With his knowledge of Washington, D.C., he became a very useful spy.

Thomas spied for the Confederacy throughout the war. Thomas knew a clerk in the Union War Department who would leave information on his desk when he went to lunch. Thomas would stroll by the clerk's desk, read the papers, and take what he learned back to Confederate military leaders.

cavalry—soldiers who travel and fight on horseback

chaplain—a religous leader who performs religious ceremonies and is an officer in the military

civilian—a person who is not in the military

Thomas wasn't always disguised as a chaplain. He changed his hair color and whiskers to suit each spying mission. To look like a Northerner, Thomas bought shoes commonly worn by Northerners. He trimmed his beard but not his bushy sideburns to give himself a popular Northern look. He even bought "short cut" tobacco used by Northerners. Thomas also found creative ways to keep sensitive information safe. For one job he found a **cobbler** who supported the South. The cobbler hollowed out the heels of some shoes worn by men Thomas was helping. Important papers were stuffed inside the heels to keep them safe.

Thomas and another man eventually hatched a plan to kidnap President Lincoln. The president often spent summer nights at the Old Soldiers' Home several miles north of the White House. Thomas learned President Lincoln's route to and from the Old Soldiers' Home and decided to kidnap him.

But before Thomas could act on his plan, the Pennsylvania **infantry** began accompanying Lincoln on his trips. Thomas never followed through with his kidnapping plan.

Years later, Thomas looked back on his spying career. He wrote, "Never will the day come when he [Thomas] will forget or regret services to the 'Cause' now 'Lost'."

cobbler—someone who makes or repairs footwear
infantry—soldiers who travel and fight on foot

ACTING THE PART

It was March 1863. An audience at Wood's Theater in Louisville, Kentucky, was enjoying a performance of the popular comedy *The Seven Sisters*. Suddenly one of the actresses stepped to the edge of the stage. She raised a wineglass and in a loud, clear voice shouted, "Here's to Jeff Davis and the Southern Confederacy!"

For a moment, the audience was shocked into silence. Kentucky was a Northern state. To shout such a toast in the second year of the Civil War was a crime.

But what better way for actress Pauline Cushman to begin her career as a Union spy?

Two days earlier, Confederate officers at Pauline's boarding house offered her $300 to toast the Confederacy in the play. The next day, Pauline reported their offer to a Union officer. He told her to make the toast and use her acting ability to create the perfect cover for a Union spy.

Pauline was immediately fired from her acting job, but began her new career as a spy. One mission in particular almost cost Pauline her life.

She was acting in Nashville, Tennessee, then occupied by Union troops. Her **spymaster**, Colonel William Truesdail, told her to slip through Confederate lines and visit five camps. She was to say she was looking for her brother, a Confederate soldier. Her real assignment was to study the enemy's defenses. Truesdail warned her to memorize everything instead of writing it down. But for reasons known only to herself, Pauline ignored his orders.

spymaster—the head of a ring of spies

Pauline's acting talents and her reputation as a Southern sympathizer helped her become friends with officers at the camps. They spoke freely around her, giving her a great deal of information.

Pauline slyly stole important papers from a young Confederate engineer. She took clothes from a young man in her boarding house and then hopped on a horse. Pauline rode into the night. She hoped to run into a Union patrol that would take her information to Nashville.

After a long ride Pauline spotted a campfire. She slid off her horse and sneaked up on four men around the fire. She hoped they were Union, but when she heard them singing a Confederate song, she jumped back on her horse and sped away. They had heard her, though, and took off after what they thought was a boy.

As she raced through the woods, she suddenly halted her horse. A man on horseback blocked her way. She warned him to move or she would shoot. He told her he was already shot and bleeding. They soon realized they were both Union supporters, and with the group of Confederate soldiers approaching, Pauline had to think fast.

She told the man to say that she had shot him. That way he would be taken as a prisoner to safety and the Confederates would be convinced she was a Southerner.

For her brave work as
a Union spy, President
Lincoln made Pauline an
honorary Union major.

Her plan worked, but Pauline was forced to return to her hotel. She tried again to get her information to the Union. She hid her notes and papers in her clothes, and a few days later headed off again for Nashville.

This time Pauline wasn't so lucky. She was caught by a Confederate scout and taken to Brigadier General Nathan Bedford Forrest's headquarters for questioning.

When a rainstorm halted their ride to headquarters, Pauline found a way to escape. The soldiers and their prisoner had taken cover in a small shack. A slave huddled fearfully nearby. Pauline gave him $10 to slip out of the house and shout "Yankees are coming!" She knew that if the small party of Confederate soldiers heard this, they would race off in fear of a large Union force.

Again her plan worked. When the soldiers heard the shout, they jumped on their horses and fled, leaving Pauline to escape. Pauline rode through the stormy night and eventually took shelter in another house. But the Confederate soldiers found her there.

Brigadier General Nathan Bedford Forrest

They took Pauline to General Braxton Bragg's headquarters in Shelbyville. Bragg ordered an investigation into the accusations against Pauline. During the investigation, papers were found in her belongings that proved she was a spy. The court sentenced her to hang and then put her in prison to await her death.

In prison Pauline became ill. She hoped the Confederates would not hang a sick woman, and she was right. Perhaps she could stay sick long enough for the Union troops to retake Shelbyville.

Just when Pauline had lost all hope, the Union army attacked. The Confederates fell back and left Pauline behind. Once behind Union lines, Pauline relayed the information she remembered. Forever after she was sorry she disobeyed her spymaster's orders.

General Braxton Bragg

FROM SLAVE TO SPY

Mary Elizabeth Bowser was born a slave on a Virginia plantation owned by John Van Lew. Van Lew's daughter, Elizabeth, hated slavery. When her father died, Elizabeth and her mother freed all the slaves. Elizabeth did a special favor for Mary. She enrolled her in the Quaker School for Negroes in Philadelphia, Pennsylvania.

When war broke out, Mary returned to Richmond. By then Elizabeth had started spying for the Union. It didn't take long for Elizabeth to decide that the best place to learn Confederate secrets was in the Confederate White House. She thought Mary was just the girl for the job.

Mary took the name "Ellen Bond," and got a job as a servant at the Confederate White House. She pretended to be an ignorant servant who could not read or write. When she poured tea for Jefferson Davis and his guests, she listened to every word they said. While sweeping the hallways, she caught bits of conversation from other rooms. When she dusted the president's office, she read everything on his desk. Everything she learned, she passed on to Elizabeth and other Union supporters.

Between 1863 and 1864, the information Mary provided greatly influenced Union decisions. By January 1865, President Davis knew there was a leak in the White House. Mary figured it was only a matter of time before she was caught. She knew she had to leave. No one knows what happened to her after the war.

Confederate White House

FACT:

In 1995 Mary Elizabeth Bowser was elected to the Military Intelligence Hall of Fame for her work as a spy during the Civil War.

BEHIND ENEMY LINES

Spencer Kellogg Brown learned about war and courage early in life. Spencer was just a boy when his father moved the family to Kansas. They settled in a community that wanted Kansas to be a slave-free state. When Spencer was in his early teens, pro-slavery men from Missouri attacked the settlement he lived in. Spencer was taken prisoner. He watched his house burn to the ground and saw friends and neighbors lying dead. Spencer was released after a few weeks, but the experience made him hate slavery and the South even more.

Before the Civil War broke out, Spencer enlisted in the Union army. Once fighting began, he joined the Union navy. The navy tried to keep the Mississippi River open as a trade route for the North. But the Confederates controlled parts of the river.

Spencer Kellogg Brown.

In January 1862 Spencer volunteered to head south into enemy territory. His goal was to find out what types of defenses the Union would face when it decided to invade. In the dead of night, Spencer and another volunteer used a small boat to take them across the Mississippi River. At dawn they pulled up alongside a Confederate steamer. They shouted and got the attention of a crew member. The crewman was surprised to see the Union sailors and took them to Captain Guthrie.

Spencer and his partner told the captain they had deserted the Union navy. Guthrie questioned them carefully. While he treated them kindly, he would not allow them to leave the ship. Eventually, they were placed under guard on a Confederate gunboat. All the while Spencer paid attention to details.

Two days later Spencer and his partner were sent ashore to New Madrid, Missouri, in Confederate territory. There the men worked for the Engineer Corps. A Confederate soldier there suspected Spencer of spying and arrested him. Spencer was forced to march a long distance. When he wasn't marching he sat on painfully thin rails all day. He was eventually transferred to another boat. During it all, Spencer tried to remember everything he saw.

After about two weeks, he won the confidence of the officers, who doubted he was a spy. Eventually, Spencer convinced the commander that he wanted to join the Confederate forces. So he received a pass to Corinth, Mississippi, where he could sign up.

Spencer joined the 1st Louisiana Volunteers and almost immediately was sent marching toward the front lines. He was terrified. "I expected every moment to be brought into a fight against my friends," he wrote.

The USS Essex was one of many gunboats patrolling the Mississippi River during the Civil War.

Before he had to fight, however, Spencer made a break for the Union line. He sneaked out of camp early one morning and quickly made his way to the Tennessee River, 1.5 miles (2.4 km) away. If he could cross it, he would be in Union territory. The freezing water weighed his clothes down so much that he couldn't swim. Spencer returned to the riverbank, stripped naked, and went back into the ice-cold water.

Spencer swam to an island in the middle of the river. He crossed the rest of the river in a dugout canoe. Spencer crawled up on the Northern side wearing only his hat. Eventually, a man gave him some clothes and food.

Once Spencer reached Union troops, they put him under guard, fearing he was a Confederate spy. However, he was quickly cleared and reported his findings to General Grant.

Spencer continued spying behind Confederate lines as the Union fought its way down the Mississippi. Spencer volunteered to sink a Confederate ferryboat hauling supplies. With 40 men, Spencer set out for the boat. They destroyed the ship.

As Spencer's boat was returning to shore two soldiers called to him. He recognized them as Union. But as soon as he went ashore, Confederates rushed out from the brush and arrested Spencer and his men. The two soldiers had been Confederate spies placed in the Union army.

Spencer was arrested and kept in prison for a year. He was found guilty of spying and sentenced to hang. Before he was hanged in Richmond on September 25, 1863, Spencer said, "My death is dark, but beyond all is light and bright."

Spencer was held at Libby Prison before his death.

SPY SISTERS

The Moon sisters had exactly what it took to be spies during the Civil War. They were fiercely independent, smart, and brave. When the war broke out, Lottie Moon Clark was 32 years old and married to Judge Jim Clark. Ginnie Moon was a 17-year-old student at the Oxford Female Institute in Ohio.

Lottie and Jim supported the Confederacy, though they lived in the North. Jim was in a Confederate spy ring called the Knights of the Golden Circle. In the summer of 1862, another member dropped by. He needed to get some papers to a Confederate general in Kentucky. But he was being followed by a Union patrol.

Lottie grabbed the papers and made her way to the city of Lexington. Playing the part of an Irish servant, she handed the papers to the first Confederate officer she saw. Her career as a spy had begun.

Meanwhile, Ginnie had decided she didn't want to stay at the school in Ohio. She begged the principal to let her leave. When he refused, Ginny shot the stars out of the American flag flying outside the school. She was immediately kicked out of school.

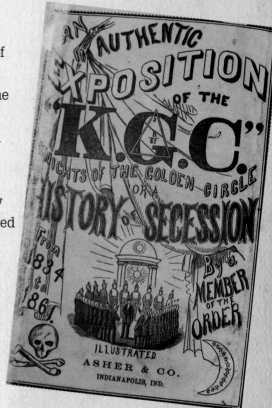

Lottie Moon Clark

Ginnie had a short stay at Lottie's house in Ohio. Then she went to live with her mother in Memphis, in the Confederate state of Tennessee. There the women nursed sick and wounded Confederate soldiers. In the summer of 1862, Memphis fell to Union troops. Ginnie began making friends with Union soldiers, hoping to gain useful information. She learned about troop movements, defenses, and supplies. To get information past the Union lines, Ginnie told the guards she was heading south to meet a boyfriend.

In December 1862, Ginnie heard that Confederate Major General Sterling Price needed to get a message to the Ohio members of the Knights of the Golden Circle. Ginnie volunteered to take the message to her brother-in-law Jim. She would take her mother along as proof of her cover story that they were simply heading north for a family reunion.

Ginnie and her mother arrived at Jim and Lottie's house without any problems. Lottie was in Canada at the time, but Jim entertained his guests for several weeks.

Major General
Sterling Price

Union agents had their eye on the Clark house, though. They knew that Jim was a member of the Circle. They planted one of their own spies in the Clark house to find out what the women were up to. But he never learned a thing. All the women seemed interested in was sewing quilts.

When it came time to head home, the women booked passage on a steamboat that ran up and down the Ohio River. They filled their trunks with quilts and went aboard.

A Union official confronted Ginnie in her room. He accused her of smuggling goods and messages to the Confederates. She would need to be searched. It was decided that a female housekeeper would search Ginnie. When the official left the room, Ginnie dipped a message from Jim for the Confederates in water and ate it.

But there was nothing she could do about her trunks. Her quilts were stuffed with packets of medicine for wounded Confederate soldiers. And when Ginnie was searched, the housekeeper found about 50 letters and more than 40 bottles of medicine hidden beneath her skirt.

Ginnie was desperate. She could think of only one person who might help her—Union General Ambrose Burnside. Years earlier, Lottie had agreed to marry Burnside, but on their wedding day, she didn't show up. Would Burnside possibly take pity on Lottie's little sister? Ginnie demanded to see him. Burnside saw her and her mother. He had no hard feelings, but decided they had to stay in custody for now.

Though Ginnie and her mother were treated very well, they were still prisoners. Several days later, a lady who called herself Mrs. Hull showed up at Burnside's residence. Burnside recognized her at once. It was Lottie Moon in disguise. She was hoping to help her mother and sister escape. Instead Lottie joined them in captivity. After several weeks, the Moon ladies were released. Lottie returned to Ohio, while Ginnie and her mother headed back to Memphis.

Union General
Ambrose Burnside

A DARING SCOUT

Archie Rowand Jr. was 17 when he joined the Union cavalry in what would soon become the state of West Virginia. One day Archie's commander asked for volunteers for extra dangerous duty. Archie looked at his friend Ike Harris, and they both stepped forward.

The duty was **scouting**. Archie and Ike put on the gray uniforms of Confederate soldiers and went behind enemy lines to gather information.

Archie knew it was dangerous work, but he made a great spy. Archie had lived in South Carolina as a child, so he could speak with a Southern accent.

In June 1863 Archie was scouting behind Confederate lines dressed as a Confederate soldier. He and three other scouts stopped at a farmhouse to eat. Two scouts stood guard outside while Archie and the other man ate. When they came out to take guard duty, their two guards were gone. A voice shouted for them to surrender.

"Are you Yanks?" Archie called out.

"No!" came the answer. Archie and his partner surrendered. Archie remembered he had a pass in his pocket identifying him as a Union scout! He needed the pass so he could get back to the Union side safely.

FACT: Being an army scout had its privileges. Scouts were able to come and go as they pleased. They were also paid in gold for information they provided.

Union scouts for the Army of the Potomac pose for a photograph.

scout—to travel ahead of a military group to gather information about the enemy

General John C. Breckenridge

The suspicious Confederates took Archie's **revolver**. At the same time, Archie slipped the pass from his pocket and slid it up his sleeve. During questioning, he told the Confederates he and his partner were couriers carrying oral messages from Confederate General John McCausland.

The man questioning Archie was Captain Hoffman. Hoffman demanded descriptions of men Archie should know if he really was in the Confederate army. Fortunately Archie had seen every one of them and gave accurate descriptions.

When Hoffman asked where Archie was from, Archie claimed to be from Weston, West Virginia. Hoffman smiled. He knew several people in Weston and told Archie to describe them. Luckily, Archie's company had camped in Weston so he knew the people Hoffman asked about.

This left Hoffman staring at Archie. The boy laughed and said, "You think I am a deserter?"

The Confederate captain shook his head. "No ... you puzzle me. You are a Southerner—You are no Yankee. I am sure of that."

With that, Hoffman gave Archie and his partner a letter to be delivered immediately to General Breckenridge, commander of the Confederate forces nearby. Archie delivered the letter instead to Union General Averell the next morning.

Union General Ulysses S. Grant never forgot Archie's moments of raw courage. In 1873 he awarded Archie the Medal of Honor.

Archie Rowand Jr.

revolver—a type of handgun that usually has five to eight cartridges in a cylinder

SOUNDING THE ALARM

As a child in Martinsburg, Virginia, Belle Boyd enjoyed climbing trees and racing her horse through the woods. She also loved school. She was a bright, mischievous student who enjoyed playing pranks.

In 1860, when Belle was 17, she moved to Washington, D.C. Belle later wrote "We ate and drank, we dined and danced … without a thought of the volcano that was seething beneath our feet." That volcano was the Civil War. When it began in 1861, Belle returned to Martinsburg. By July she was nursing wounded Confederate soldiers at local hospitals.

When Union troops overtook the town on July 3, 1861, they stormed into Belle's home, taking whatever they wanted. To make matters worse, the Union soldiers tried to hang the Union flag atop Belle's house. Her mother refused. A soldier lunged at Belle's mother and insulted her. In an instant, Belle shot the man. He died a short time later.

At this time President Lincoln was trying to stop more states from leaving the Union. He didn't want trouble or unnecessary bloodshed. Historians think this is why the Union officers who investigated the shooting agreed with Belle that the shooting was justified.

Belle Boyd around
the time of the
Civil War

In May 1862 Belle was visiting relatives in Front Royal, Virginia. Front Royal was in Union hands. Confederate General Stonewall Jackson was marching his army north to retake it. The Union had supplies and ammunition stored in Front Royal. They planned to protect them at all costs.

Belle heard that at least five different Union forces were going to meet up and take on Jackson's army. She knew that if Jackson got the Union supplies before the extra Union forces arrived, he could defeat them.

Battle of Front Royal,
May 1862

On May 23, a servant rushed into the home Belle was staying at, shouting that the rebels were coming. Belle ran into the street. She had written down the information about the Union supplies in Front Royal and the coming Union troops. Belle asked a group of Southerners in the street if they would take the message to General Jackson. They all refused.

Belle later claimed that she didn't even think twice. "I put on a white sunbonnet, and started at a run down the street."

Belle charged through the
Union line. She heard bullets
whistle past her. An artillery
shell exploded near her and
knocked her to the ground. She
got up and continued running
toward the Confederate line.

Belle later wrote, "Hope,
fear, the love of life, and the
determination to serve my country
to the last" kept her running as she
never had before.

As she neared the Southern line,
Belle took off her white bonnet and
waved it wildly. She gestured for
the soldiers to attack Front Royal
quickly. The Confederates cheered
and raced forward. Shortly
after, an aide of General
Jackson's and an old friend of
Belle's, Harry Douglas, rode up.

Belle gave Douglas the
information she'd been trying
to relay. She told him to attack
quickly and secure the bridges.
Douglas rode off to tell Jackson.
The Confederates won the battle
that day.

WHEN THE FIGHTING STOPPED

On Sunday, April 9, 1865, Confederate General Robert E. Lee surrendered his army to Union General Ulysses S. Grant. The event took place at the McLean farmhouse at Appomattox Court House in Virginia. Another month passed before the fighting completely ended. About 750,000 Americans—soldiers and civilians—had died. Slavery was officially outlawed everywhere in the United States. The states were reunited under one government.

Civil War spies helped shape the outcome of the war. If Betty Duvall hadn't delivered Rose Greenhow's message, the Union may have won at Bull Run. The war may have ended sooner. If Belle Boyd hadn't relayed her message to Stonewall Jackson, the Union could have crushed the Confederate army at Front Royal.

General Robert E. Lee, 1863

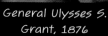
General Ulysses S. Grant, 1876

Spies also destroyed enemy supplies. Spencer Kellogg Brown helped blow up the biggest Confederate gunboat on the Mississippi River. Archie Rowand Jr. blew up bridges that the Confederates could have used to move north. Without the hundreds of known and unknown Civil War spies, the course of the war may have been very different.

FACT:
For the first time in American history, spies took to the air during the Civil War. Both the Confederate and Union armies sent people up in balloons to view the land and to spot troop movements. The drawback was that the other side could easily spot the balloons.

GLOSSARY

cavalry (KA-vuhl-ree)—soldiers who travel and fight on horseback

chaplain (CHAP-lin)—a religous leader who performs religious ceremonies and is an officer in the military

cipher (SYE-fuhr)—a code that uses letters or symbols to represent letters of the alphabet

civilian (si-VIL-yuhn)—a person who is not in the military

cobbler (KOB-lur)—someone who makes or repairs footwear

Confederate (kuhn-FED-ur-uht)—describes people from the 11 southern states that left the United States to form the Confederate States of America

infantry (IN-fuhn-tree)—soldiers who travel and fight on foot

post (POHST)—a military base where soldiers are stationed or trained

revolver (rih-VOL-vur)—a type of handgun that usually has five to eight cartridges in a cylinder

scout (SKOUT)—to travel ahead of a military group to gather information about the enemy

smuggle (SMUHG-uhl)—to bring something or someone into or out of a country illegally

spymaster (SPYE-mas-tuhr)—the head of a ring of spies

spy ring (SPYE RING)—a group of spies working together for a common goal

Union (YOON-yuhn)—the United States of America; also the Northern states that fought against the Southern states in the Civil War

READ MORE

Jarrow, Gail. *Lincoln's Flying Spies: Thaddeus Lowe and the Civil War Balloon Corps.* Honesdale, Pa.: Calkins Creek, 2010.

Lassieur, Allison, and Matt Doeden. *The Civil War Experience: An Interactive History Adventure.* You Choose History. North Mankato, Minn.: Capstone Press, 2013.

Moss, Marissa. *Nurse, Soldier, Spy: The Story of Sarah Edmonds, a Civil War Hero.* New York: Abrams Books for Young Readers, 2011.

INTERNET SITES

FactHound offers a safe, fun way to find Internet sites related to this book. All of the sites on FactHound have been researched by our staff.

Here's all you do:

Visit *www.facthound.com*

Type in this code: 9781429699761

INDEX